IMAGES
of America

JOHNSON

This panoramic view of Johnson was taken from the hill above 71 McCuin Drive. Buildings include the United Church parsonage and Mattie Baker's home. Visible are the Woolen Mill, United Church, Chesamore Building, the Grist Mill, V. Despault block, and Pop Odell's. Also note the Waters, Hill, Alumni, and Martinetti Houses; the home of Phillip Smith, and Donald Manley; and farm houses in the distance. (Courtesy of Gordon Smith.)

ON THE COVER: Logs are being prepared to enter the Parker & Stearns sawmill, long located on River Street East. Jack Amidon uses a pike pole to handle the logs in the mill pond and direct them to the skid-way of the mill. The mill pond helped cleanse the logs before sawing. (Courtesy of Mills Collection.)

IMAGES
of America

JOHNSON

Johnson Historical Society

ARCADIA
PUBLISHING

Copyright © 2011 by Johnson Historical Society
ISBN 978-1-5316-5042-1

Published by Arcadia Publishing
Charleston, South Carolina

Library of Congress Control Number: 2011924175

For all general information, please contact Arcadia Publishing:
Telephone 843-853-2070
Fax 843-853-0044
E-mail sales@arcadiapublishing.com
For customer service and orders:
Toll-Free 1-888-313-2665

Visit us on the Internet at www.arcadiapublishing.com

CONTENTS

ACKNOWLEDGMENTS

The Johnson Historical Society was established in November 2006 when the board of selectmen endorsed the organization and appointed a board of directors. For that action, we thank chairman Eric Osgood, Blaine Delisle, Franklin "Rocky" Hooper, Brad Reed, and Howard Romero. With an organization in place, community members very generously donated artifacts and pictures to the society's collection. Many of those pictures are included and noted in this book. Additionally, a number of folks helped by sharing their memories, providing a wealth of information, as we captioned the photographs for which we thank: Marie Boisonneault, Frank Dodge, Farnum Emery, Linda Jones, Jollie Parker, Helen Perkins, Richard and Helaine Perkins, Donald Manley, Andre Nadeau, Bernard and Janet Sheltra, Robert Sinclair, Amy Thompson, Dean West, and Alice Whiting. Not only for his technical expertise about photographs but also his ability and patience in sharing his knowledge with us when we needed help, we thank Sherlock Terry at Johnson State College. Finally, we extend our heartfelt appreciation to all members of the Johnson community, who support the historical society's purpose to study, record, collect, and preserve the history of Johnson and its environs.

There are four books that provide a great deal of historical information:

Baker, Mattie W. and the Oread Literary Club. *History of the Town of Johnson, Vermont. 1784–1907.* Burlington: Free Press Printing Company, 1907.

Smalley, Margaret T.; Hill, Ethel S.; May, Helen; Rexford, Zillah, Chitwood. *History of Johnson Vermont 1961.* Essex Publishing Company, Essex, Vermont. 1962.

Raymond, Kenneth. *The History of Johnson State College: 1828–1984.* Johnson State College, 1985.

Graff, Nancy Price. *A Perspective on the History and Architecture of Johnson, Vermont.* Historic Preservation Program, Department of History, University of Vermont in cooperation with the Vermont Studio School and Colony. 1990.

INTRODUCTION

Johnson, Vermont, lies in the heart of Lamoille County on 30,656 acres. It is 45-plus square miles of varied topography. The township was first granted to Joseph Brown in 1780. Because of his failure to pay grant fees and his unknown whereabouts, another grant was made to William Samuel Johnson in 1782. After some controversy about the change, a charter was given in 1792 to Mr. Johnson with the name of Johnson.

Samuel Eaton is believed to be the first permanent settler in 1784. By 1792, Johnson had been settled in several different areas by mostly self-sustaining farms, though a small grist mill had been established along the Gihon River by two brothers named McConnell, who came from New Hampshire. By the early 1800s, the center of the town was developing along the junction of the Gihon and Lamoille Rivers in the area now known as Johnson Village. As this movement took place, the development of an industrial base also was built along the rivers and within the village. Some enterprises in the village from 1820 through the 1890s were an oil (flax seed) mill, rake factory, distillery, potash factory, chair factory, tin shops, a grist mill, blacksmiths, a hat factory, and a carriage shop.

Around the turn of the century, Johnson began to transform into a growing modern community. While one of the earliest town meetings on March 4, 1789, elected a board of selectmen, it was after November 5, 1894, when the village was incorporated, that significant municipal development followed. The electric system with a power station became operational in January 1895. Throughout that year the grammar school, the Sterling Hose Company (the forerunner of the Johnson Fire Department), and the public library all opened and the water system became operational. All were owned and operated by the village or town government.

It was during this same period that much industry developed. Around 1907, Parker and Stearns expanded its lumber manufacturing to the milling of hardwood flooring and began shipping to national markets. The woolen mill expanded to manufacture woolen garments. Talc was discovered and a plant was built for its processing. A rake factory was producing 50,000 rakes annually and the tub factory was shipping its wares nationally. Meanwhile, the retail shops were growing. While there had been as many as 17 one-room schools throughout town, they were consolidating, sending their students to the new, larger village school. There were hotels for travelers, including the Allen Stand and the Everett Hotel. In addition there were smaller facilities such as the Oasis and the Townley cabins. The railroad was busy, which encouraged Leonard Knight to construct a new store, the Nye Block, at the southwest corner of Main and Railroad Streets in anticipation of a new railroad junction in town. The railroad junction never materialized. However, the Vermont Transit Company ran a bus service with Johnson as a junction with runs to Burlington, St. Albans, Montreal, Newport, St. Johnsbury, Montpelier, and Portland, Maine for many years. Some of these businesses continue to operate today, although changed somewhat in their function.

The middle of the 20th century saw changes taking place as some of the manufacturing processes were replaced by modern technology. Johnson Normal School expanded and ultimately became

Johnson State College, offering a four-year liberal arts program in addition to its traditional teacher education curriculum. The Vermont Electric Cooperative, responsible for bringing electricity to many rural areas, established its headquarters in town in 1950. Laraway School moved to Johnson in 1974. It is an independent school that provides a structured environment for students in fourth through 12th grades. The Vermont Studio Center, with artist and writer residency programs, was created in 1984. It has remodeled and preserved 30 historic buildings to build the campus by the Gihon River. Other small businesses have been introduced to replace older ones. The Albert S. Nadeau Aggregate business was established in 1945. The plant was operational by May 1946 supplying all the processed aggregates for the Green River Dam in Hyde Park.

People make up the fabric of a community. Throughout this book are pictures of farmers, mill workers, miners, merchants, sugar makers, homemakers, teachers and so many more who were the foundation of Johnson as we know it today. Church and service organizations played a significant role in the celebrations that appear in the photographs as townspeople acknowledge their military men and women at Memorial Day Parades over the years. Also, crowds gather to celebrate the nation's bicentennial in 1976. Young people are seen enjoying swimming and skiing, Beverly Stackpole celebrates her sixth birthday, and teenagers participate in a variety of athletic pursuits.

Visitors to Johnson have come perhaps for the educational opportunities provided by the Vermont Studio Center or Johnson State College. Some visit as they hike the Long Trail needing rest and refreshments. Others visit various stores such as the Woolen Mill for warm clothing and Butternut Mountain Store for maple products. They may be traveling the Vermont Route 15 corridor on their way to one of our neighboring ski areas (Smugglers and Stowe) and find that Johnson is the place to stop.

Johnson evolved from an early, self-sufficient, agricultural town to a diverse community depending on business and industry, education, the arts, and agriculture as its economic engine. Farms, which were numerous in the early part of the century, were greatly reduced in number by the 1960s. In the early years, sheep farms were numerous but by the middle of the century they had greatly diminished. Dairy farming experienced a similar decline. The farmlands have been put to different uses; however, maple sugaring has continued to be an important product.

The growth and evolution of Johnson from the late 19th century through the 20th century should become clear in the pages of this book. We have endeavored to illustrate some of the hardships and the joys faced by those who walked before us. We hope readers feel a sense of our community as they get a view of the people, places, businesses, and events that created the character and strength of the community we enjoy today. We also hope readers will use this work to refresh memories, understand the past, enjoy the contributions of many; and for those unfamiliar with our town, to become acquainted with the community we call Johnson, Vermont.

One

Heart of
the Community

Approaching Johnson from the East is a winding road down Gulf Hill known as the gateway to the village. Through the years there has been little change to this roadway due to the steep banks on both sides. Winter snow and ice can make this road difficult to travel. (Courtesy of the Mills Collection.)

A town meeting is held on the first Tuesday of March. In the early days it was held in the town hall, now known as the Lowe Lecture Hall. These meetings were well attended with the voters sitting on the main floor and non-voters in the balcony. On the stage are moderator William Sinclair (standing) and town clerk Roger Richards (seated). (Courtesy of the Mills Collection.)

The Board of Civil Authority for the town of Johnson is sitting at the back of the stage at town hall, counting town meeting day ballots. The members are, from left to right, Watts Shattuck (back to camera), Kenneth Hopkins, Earl Butler, Joel Hooper and Frank Dodge. (Courtesy of the Mills Collection.)

10

St. John's Catholic Church at 32 St. John's Street is as it appeared for the wedding of Laurie West to Barney McClean in 1981. The church was constructed in 1948–1949 on land purchased from Frank LeMay's farm and under the direction of its first pastor, Rev. Omer Dufault. The interior has remained essentially unchanged since its inaugural mass on April 19, 1999. (Courtesy of Laurie McClean.)

Three long-time residents attend a function at St. John's Catholic Church. Raoul West (center) was a 45-year employee of the talc mill. Lucille West (left) is known for her work at the graded school and Johnson State College. Ceil Miller (right) was a hairdresser from her School Street home into the 1990s. (Courtesy of Laurie McClean.)

The Cold Spring was deeded to the town by Mattie Baker and served as the village's fresh water supply after the flood of 1927. The stonework surrounding the spring was one of the many accomplishments of Johnson's Community League. The spring continues to provide drinking water for many people today. (Courtesy of the Mills Collection.)

The first church of the Nazarene began as the First Pentecostal Church of Johnson in 1904 and was moved to the new church at 143 Lower Main East in 1907. It was remodeled in 1923 with the addition of a tower to the front. When the church moved to a new location outside the village, this building became privately owned. (Courtesy of Robert Whiting.)

The Congregational Church was built around 1850. Constructed in the Greek Revival style, the church facade became a visual attraction on Main Street. Beautiful stained glass windows on three sides of this structure contributed to its visual impact. The Methodist and Congregational churches united in 1930 to become the United Church. Unfortunately, the church burned in February 1969. The Methodist parsonage at 20 McCuin Drive became the United Church parsonage. It is now home to Engel's Sewing Machine Repairs and apartments. Pictured below, local businessman Delmar Barrows presented a pipe organ, the only one in town, to the church in 1927. (Courtesy of the Mills Collection.)

Early church leaders of the United Church gather at the Phyllis Titus home. From left to right are (seated) Clara Hopkins, Clara Lowe, Phyllis Titus, and Ann Mills; (standing) A. Ritchie Lowe, Kenneth Hopkins, and unidentified. The Reverend A. Ritchie Lowe was pastor of the United Church from 1932 to 1947. (Courtesy of Nichols Collection.)

After the United Church burned in 1969, a planning committee for building a new church was formed. In the Masonic Temple Lodge Room are, from left to right, Howard Hill, Janice Rushford, N. Dean Rowe, Florence Rowe, and Theodore Cromack. The Masonic Temple was used temporarily for church services. (Courtesy of the United Church Collection.)

Under the direction of Jollie Parker, the United Church choir, with Rachel Smith at the piano, is rehearsing for services at the Masonic Temple. Among the choir members are, from left to right, (first row) Jane Jeffreys, Alice Barber, unidentified, Alice Gross, and Hal Parker; (second row) Donald Barber and William Schoonmaker. (Courtesy of the United Church Collection.)

Once a site for the new United Church was chosen, the congregation paraded from the Masonic Temple down Main Street for the ground-breaking. After passing the Landmark Building, the parade turned right to the new site. Among those marching are Norman Scott, Hubert and Florence Beard, Sybil Sweet, Laura Green, Mary Sinclair, Clara Mason, Helen Perkins, and Rene Godin. (Courtesy of the United Church Collection.)

The ground-breaking for the new United Church was a special occasion for many people. With shovels in hand, Hubert Beard and Dorothy Richards remove a layer of snow and frozen soil as a first step in the building of the new church. Also pictured are Mary Sinclair, Harry Parker, an unidentified youth holding the banner, and Rev. Park Dickerson. (Courtesy of the United Church Collection.)

This building, financed by selling pews at $100 each, was dedicated as a Methodist Church in 1855. In 1930, when the Methodist and Congregational Churches united, it became Johnson's post office. The sanctuary, used occasionally, remained upstairs with the post office on the lower level. The building is presently owned by the Vermont Studio Center. (Courtesy of the Mills Collection.)

This picture shows Main Street following a snowstorm around 1930. Notable is the snow-covered streetlight at the top. Other highlights are the Grand Union with a barber pole indicating the barbershop on the lower level and the Route 15 sign. While the street appears to have been plowed, snow removal is certainly not up to today's standards. (Courtesy of the Mills Collection.)

Main Street bridge traffic is blocked by an overturned milk truck in the 1940s. The truck reportedly struck the bridge while trying to avoid striking a child who had used the inside of the bridge rails while playing hide and seek. The point of impact was visible until the bridge was demolished. Note the dog enjoying spilled milk. (Courtesy of the Johnson Historical Society.)

This view of Main Street is looking east. The house on the lower left of the picture provided housing for principals of Johnson Grade School for many years on this tree-lined street. Two sleighs drawn by horses are shown with the one to the right drinking from the watering tub. (Courtesy of Linda Jones.)

Pictured is an early 1900s overview of Johnson village. Various landmarks include Nye Block, the opera house and town hall, Chesamore, United Church, and the Masonic Temple with the town clock. Looking east beyond the village are open pasturelands, which afforded a view of the community below. (Courtesy of Linda Jones.)

18

There is no movie theater in Johnson today; however, in the 1920s, films were shown in the upper level of a building near the Pearl Street bridge. Shown here is Georgia Scott Jones in front of the billboard on Main Street advertising the upcoming Saturday show. (Courtesy of Linda Jones.)

William LaPorte operated a garage that later burned near the Pearl Street bridge. He also operated a blacksmith's shop providing shoes for the horses of farmers and village folk. He is shown here in his retirement years giving a demonstration of his blacksmithing skills to visitors at the Shelburne Museum. (Courtesy of Linda Jones.)

19

Approaching the twin bridges on Pearl Street from Main Street, on the left, is a building that housed a blacksmith shop, apartments, and, upstairs, a movie theater. On the right is C. H. Stearns & Son gristmill. Standing on the bridge's walkway are Bunty Lowe and Gene Sargent. (Courtesy of Mildred Sargent, Doris Stearns photographer.)

Ken Hopkins (far right) is busy at the bench in the town garage located off Pearl Street behind the town gym. Ken is working on a track roller from the town's crawler, used primarily for snow removal, probably after a long, hard winter. Another roller on the bench awaits his attention while the rest of the town crew is busy at various shop tasks. (Courtesy of the Nichols Collection.)

20

Originally built as a store, this building sits at the corner of School and Pearl Streets. Homer Barrows was proprietor of a store there, followed by Girdon Odell, known to many as "Pop." From 1954 to 1957, a first and second grade class, with Elizabeth Parsons teaching, occupied the building. Today, it has been converted into apartments. (Courtesy of Johnson State College Alumni Archives.)

Clay Hill, which extends from Pearl Street, had at one time several houses that have since been demolished. Trees and brush have now taken their place. On the left side of the road there are still several residences. The main entrance to Johnson State College is a short distance above on Clay Hill. (Courtesy of the Johnson Historical Society.)

The dwelling at 285 Clay Hill is one of Johnson's early buildings and was occupied in the mid-1800s by Dexter Whiting. He had the town clock installed in the Baptist church and donated it to the town in 1884–1885. It has been said that he sited the clock so that it could be seen from his house. (Courtesy of the Smith family.)

Johnson has always had a number of sole proprietor businesses. Photographer Gary Smith captured the work of Robert W. Frey, a registered land surveyor, as he surveys the property of Philip and Rachel Smith at 285 Clay Hill. The home on this property is one of Johnson's oldest structures. (Courtesy of Gary Smith.)

In this early view of School Street are, from left to right, the Grange hall, the American Legion hall, and the Odell buildings. Across the street is Hill House and a house with extensive barns. The cornfield in the foreground, perhaps tended by students, is on the hillside near some college dormitories. (Courtesy of Linda Jones.)

The Johnson Grange No. 349 building dominates the left side of School Street in this picture taken from above the Legion Field. Other buildings include, from left to right, the American Legion hall and the Girdon "Pop" Odell block. Note on the telephone pole the fire siren that rang at noon and served as a warning for a fire in town. (Courtesy of the Nichols Collection.)

Members of the Johnson Grange in the 1940s are, from left to right, (first row) Smith Davis, Harry Stiles, Ada Stiles, and Emmett Sweet; (second row) Wayland Mills, Earl Butler, Phillip French, William Sinclair, Franklin Hooper, and Lawrence Sinclair; (third row) Roger Richards, Roy Cunningham, George Whitney, Ronald Hutchins, Malcolm Mudgett, Fay Frappier, and Floyd Ellsworth. (Courtesy of the Johnson Historical Society.)

HICKS' COMMISSION SALES CO.

Merrisville, Vt.
Sale Every Wednesday,
Home of a Square Deal

Dial 4531
at 2 P.M. Dial

STERLING TRUST CO.
Johnson, Vermont
BEST PLACE TO BORROW
YOUR BANK
BEST PLACE TO SAVE
Member Federal Deposit Insurance Corporation

Johnson, Vermont
Business Guide
1 9 4 9

Howard P. Hill
FURNITURE
FLOOR COVERING
BOTTLE GAS

Parker & Stearns, Inc.
Manufacturers and Wholesale Dealers in
KILN DRIED HARDWOOD FLOORING
LUMBER
Main Office and Mills
Johnson, Vermont
Telephone 20-2

The Johnson, Vermont, business guide was published by Grange No. 349 in 1949. In addition to the advertisements for Johnson and other Lamoille County businesses, it included a listing of the town and village officers, the bus schedule, and fire signals. (Courtesy of Linda Jones.)

Hubert Beard established recreation areas for community use on his property at 299 School Street. The upper picture is Beard's swimming hole on the banks of the Gihon River, which also included a picnic area. The depth of the water was increased by the tub factory dam below the site, making the use of a diving board possible. Below is the ski slope and rope tow he built in his yard and operated for free to the community during the 1950s and early 1960s. Hubert Beard was known for his ability to build and fix most anything. (Above, courtesy of Marie Boissoneault; below, courtesy of Alan Beard.)

This playground, located at the Beard's swimming hole, provided space for a variety of activities. Children could enjoy bike riding, horseshoes, or playing hide and seek among the trees as well as having a picnic with their family. On rainy days, the pavilion offered shelter. (Courtesy of the Mills Collection.)

The Power House Bridge was built in 1872, when School Street was opened from Pearl Street to Route 100C, across the Gihon River. The single span covered bridge survived the 1927 flood. It was restored in 1960 with cement abutments and other repairs. Heavy snow destroyed the bridge in 2000. Two years later, the bridge was rebuilt using timber from the town's forests. (Courtesy of the Mills Collection.)

Viewed from the beginning of Stearns Street (Route 100C) around the early 1900s is the dirt road used for travel to North Hyde Park before construction of the Power House Bridge. As with many streets in Johnson at this time, trees lined the road. On the left corner is the Whiting-Hill Cemetery. (Courtesy of Linda Jones.)

The Scribner Bridge crosses the Gihon River on Rocky Road in East Johnson. The former Mudgett farm is partially visible in the background. The open fields in the background provided pasture for cows and, more recently, for fallow deer. This covered bridge is still in use today. (Courtesy of the Johnson Historical Society.)

This view of Railroad Street looking south from the Main Street intersection was taken after the new concrete paved roadway and cement sidewalk were installed, likely in the mid-1920s. The "silent policeman" or dummy divides the intersection for safe travel and also helps to discourage corner cutting by drivers. (Courtesy of Linda Jones.)

Pictured here is the home of Dr. and Mrs. Edgar Scott on Railroad Street. He was a veterinarian who treated animals of all sizes. He went to farms to treat larger animals and smaller animals were brought to the kennels in his barn. He retired in 1958. (Courtesy of Linda Jones.)

Standing in front of their house are Edgar and Alma Scott. In addition to his veterinarian work, Doctor Scott was deputy sheriff in town for more than 20 years. Due to the respect people had for him, he was able to keep the peace with few problems. He also served in the Vermont House of Representatives. Alma stayed home to look after the animals and the doctor's business. (Courtesy of Linda Jones.)

While some children might have had ponies to pull their carts, Georgia Scott Jones (1909–2006) had a goat named Billy Gruff. A lifelong resident of Johnson, she graduated from Johnson Normal School and taught school locally, including the fourth grade at Johnson Elementary School. Later as librarian, she helped adults and youngsters select books at the Johnson Public Library. (Courtesy of Linda Jones.)

Charles Stearns donated land on Railroad Street for construction of the Johnson Public Library. The Oread Literary Club, with assistance from citizens, spearheaded the project, which was completed in 1909. The new library featured the installation of a card catalogue and a new system of charging. The 1914 town report states that "as many as 100 books are loaned daily." (Courtesy of Linda Jones.)

Johnson's Oread Literary Club was founded by Mattie Baker and Clara Farrington. In addition to maintaining the Library in its early years, the members published two town histories. As seen in this picture, the club established a historical room in the basement of the library. Many of the artifacts preserved by the club are now part of the Johnson Historical Society's Collection. (Courtesy of the Mills Collection.)

30

Twenty-eight cords of firewood were cut, split, and stacked in the backyard of the William Sladyk home on January 23, 1983. The Wood Bee was organized by neighbors Robert and Donna Laraway. The logs and trucks were donated by Howard Manosh, with equipment, labor, and food coming from Manchester's Sawmill, the Vermont Electric Cooperative, and local churches. Mary Sladyk remembers that pickup trucks stretched from the Railroad Street Bridge to Main Street as more than 100 people were part of the Wood Bee. She continues to be appreciative of the community's response, which generated the wood supply that heated her home, "four cords per year for seven years, enough time to educate my five children." Handling the chainsaws in the lower picture are Robert Laraway (left) and Malcolm Mudgett. (Courtesy of Mary Sladyk.)

The stately Waterman house located at 297 Railroad Street is one of the oldest houses in town. Araunah Waterman bought 1,200 acres of land for 4,000 Spanish silver dollars around 1800. Several generations of Watermans lived in the residence until William Tracy, a local lawyer, purchased the property c. 1900. It is presently owned by Dale and Rhoda Mingledorff. (Courtesy of the Mills Collection.)

This bridge was located on Waterman Road about two and a half miles south of Johnson village. The approach in the upper end of the bridge had stringers under the floor, while the rest of the bridge was supported by trusses. The covered bridge was in use until the 1980s when vibrations from a truck moving through the bridge caused the upper structure to collapse. (Courtesy of the Mills Collection.)

It was common for high waters of the Gihon and Lamoille Rivers to invade Lower Main Street. This scene is the curve in the road at the current fire station and shows the house that was demolished for construction of the current municipal building. The site was raised to an elevation above the flood plain. (Courtesy of the Mills Collection.)

Leaving the village, traveling west, the road took a very scenic route along the bend of the tranquil Lamoille River. In the background, notice the mainly open hillside and the bustling manufacturing facility of Eastern Magnesia Talc Company. To accommodate the increasing Route 15 traffic, this ambling drive was straightened through a rock cut to enhance traffic flow. (Courtesy of Dary Sheehy.)

The well-known Long Trail runs through Johnson providing some rugged hiking trails and overnight shelters. This Sterling Pond cabin was built of balsam logs in 1926. In 1913 a Mount Sterling section of the Green Mountain Club was formed in Johnson. In September 1970, the Sterling Section was successfully re-established and continues to this day. (Courtesy of the Nichols Collection.)

During its active years, the Grange established a picnic area on Route 15 West past the West Settlement Road. Used by local families and travelers, there are some who still remember grilling hot dogs and hamburgers over the open fire. Another community project was the publication of a cookbook, *Johnson's Treasure of Personal Recipes*, in 1952. (Courtesy of the Mills Collection.)

34

Ithiel Falls Camp Meetings have been held annually at the 3662 Hogback Road campsite since 1899. Founded by Methodist minister and evangelist Ithiel Johnson the site along the banks of the Lamoille River offers an aesthetic, as well as religious experience for families. In the above picture, the tabernacle on the left is where meetings were held morning, afternoon, and evening. Originally, people were housed in tents, then in 1930, dormitory row was added (below). Some families stayed in cabins while young people were lodged in the dormitory. Camp meetings continue to be held each August. (Courtesy of Linda Jones.)

Four Whiting brothers sat for their portrait in 1897. They are, from left to right, Freeman, Zachariah, Almon, and Arthur. At least two of them settled and farmed on Clay Hill: Zachariah on the family farm at 1775 Clay Hill and Almon at the intersection of Codding Hollow and Swamp Roads. Freeman and Arthur also lived in Johnson for a short time. (Courtesy of Alice Whiting.)

Waterman Lodge No. 83 was chartered on June 11, 1868. In 1919, the Baptist church was purchased and given by Charles Stearns to the lodge for its new home. A large number of distinguished men with their ceremonial goat stand in front of the Masonic Temple c. 1920. This building continues today to be the home of the Masons and the Eastern Star. (Courtesy of Stephen Engel.)

The Johnson Home Demonstration group met regularly at various homes. The county extension Home Economics agent attended many meetings bringing research related to homemaking. Enjoying a gathering at the Grange picnic grounds in 1960 are, from left to right, Mildred Sargent, Dorise West, Madge Thompson, Rhoda Sears, Elizabeth Robbins (home demonstration agent), Mrs. Shattuck, Ola Walker, Vera Bishop, Nina Sherbert, and Sophie Frazier. (Courtesy of the Milo Collection.)

When Beverly Stackpole Webster turned six, around 1945, she had a gala birthday party with her friends. Pictured are, from left to right, Bobby Emerson, Nancy Mills, Janet Smalley, Tresa Burnor, Eleanor Stewart, Kay Benway, Darlene Douglass, Laura Jones, and Beverly Stackpole. It appears that they are in her yard with a view of the backsides of houses on Pearl Street. (Courtesy of the Johnson Historical Society.)

Seven beagle puppies enjoy the attention of children in Marion Prescott's yard, which was on Main Street, where the municipal building stands today. From left to right are Julie Byrne, Julie LaChance, Cindy Casavant, Jackie West, Debbie Casavant, Laurie West, Vanesa Lumbra, and Julie West. The Landmark Building is in the background. (Courtesy of Laurie McClean.)

Sybil Glee Davis Sweet (1892–1991) was one of Johnson's longest living native daughters. Though she lived most of her adult life at 218 Lower Main Street West, she had a vivid memory of life and people from all over town. She was active with the United Church, Johnson Grange, and many other local groups, as well as with her daughter Phyllis Jewett, a community historian. (Courtesy of Martha Corey.)

Roger Jones was well known as a honeybee keeper. As he is approaching the hives, he is dressed with his bee veil and carrying the bee smoker. The veil is worn to protect his face. The smoker is used to excite the bees and consequently protects the beekeeper as he works with the hive. Roger sold honey, both comb and liquid, to individuals and stores in the area. Below, in this 1941 picture, Jones demonstrates his fondness for honeybees by allowing live bees to land on his chest and hands. (Courtesy of Linda Jones.)

Franklin "Red" Hooper, born in Johnson, wore many hats. He served the state for more than 40 years as a game warden. Over the years he was a Johnson selectmen, a justice of the peace, and a town service officer. When the campaign picture (left) was taken in the fall of 1988, he had been a member of the Vermont House of Representatives for eight terms, was the oldest House member, and the fourth senior in years served. His motto was "The Most Good for the Most People." Shown below, he is in the library of the elementary school talking with the students. (Left, courtesy of Linda Jones; below, courtesy of Martha Corey.)

Natalie "Nat" Hawley Jones, well known for her civic activities, is shown perhaps in the 1960s. Nat and her husband, L.L. Jones, were long-time proprietors of Jones' IGA while raising their three children. Nat was active as a school director and busy with her church activities until her retirement from Johnson State College where she was a dormitory "house mother." (Courtesy of United Church Collection.)

Joyce Balch Conger is being interviewed by her grandson Jesse Conger when students at the elementary school were learning about life in Johnson in the early days. Friends remember her bowling in the winter and golfing whenever the courses were open. They are descendents of Georgia Balch, the famous Johnson artist and Charles Stearns, a businessman. (Courtesy of Martha Corey.)

Zach Whiting, previously a mail carrier in Waterville, moved to Johnson in 1952 to take on a longer route. The first task of the morning was to sort the mail into each box holder's pigeonhole. Some will remember deliveries by him on Ober Hill, Clay Hill, and surrounding areas. (Courtesy of Linda Jones.)

After serving as a clerk, Kenneth Neill was appointed postmaster on May 3, 1955. Seen here in the lower level of the Methodist church after it was converted into a post office, he is using one of the many stamps necessary to process the outgoing mail. This was before letter sorters and cancelling machines. (Courtesy of Linda Jones.)

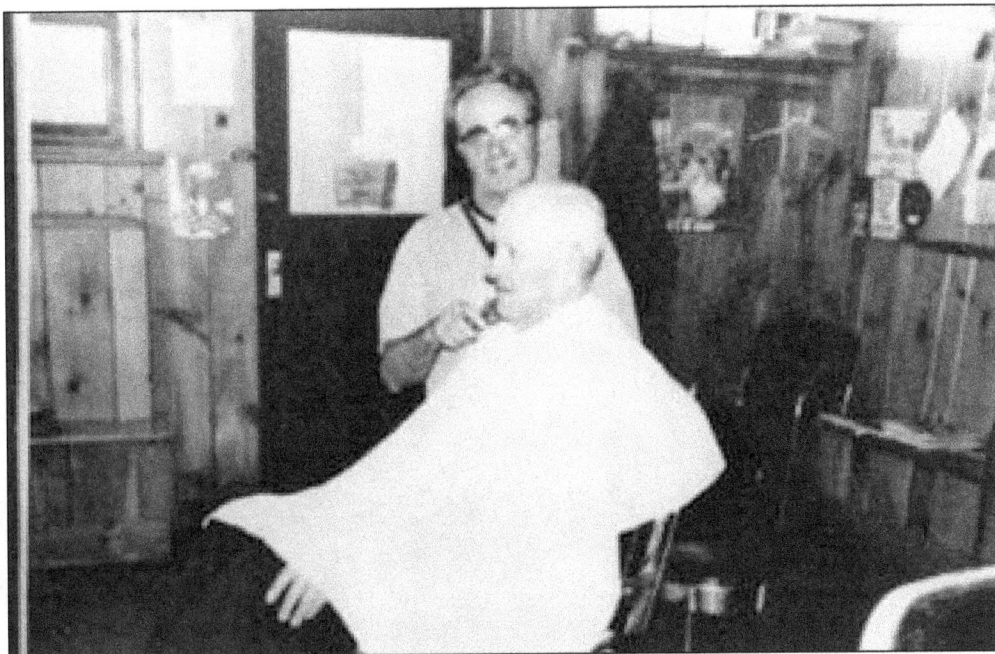

Downstairs, below the Plum and Main Restaurant was a barbershop operated by Roger Miller. Roger took care of men's barbering needs while his wife Ceil tended to the hairdressing needs of the ladies at her in-home shop on School Street. Pictured is Grover Perkins getting a haircut. (Courtesy of Helaine Perkins.)

Military service was common in many Johnson families. In 1953, Marvin Sinclair, son of Lawrence and Madeline Sinclair, returned home on leave to the family farm at 590 Rocky Road after serving on Okinawa while in the Air Force. Pictured with Marvin are his little sister Linda Sinclair Jones and her neighborhood friend Donna Mudgett Leach. (Courtesy of Linda Jones.)

A Johnson band in the mid-1800s is perhaps preparing for a concert in the bandstand in front of the building presently known as the Masonic Temple. Band members include Andy Partlow, George Partlow, Jed Pearl, Frank Woods, Fred Holmes, William Sandon, Ward Waters, Volnay Witherell, Jess Witherell, John Burnham, and Jay Partlow. (Courtesy of Helen Perkins.)

Memorial Day parades were an important part of Johnson's culture. A community band and Johnson veterans led this parade. They were followed by school children as they marched up Main Street to the Whiting-Hill Cemetery. Local residents lined the sidewalks and sat in cars to applaud and honor the parade participants. (Courtesy of the Mills Collection.)

This 1946 Memorial Day parade was a celebration of the end of World War II. A very large group of veterans participated. Following the veterans are school children as they proceed up Main Street to Railroad Street and Lamoille View Cemetery. (Courtesy of the Johnson Historical Society.)

In the 1954 Memorial Day parade, Charles Conger, Kenneth Neill and Roger Miller march past the Nye Block on Railroad Street as the parade moves to the Lamoille View Cemetery. These three men are representative of the 163 Johnson men and women who proudly served their country during World War II. (Courtesy of Marie Boissoneault.)

Leading the 1961 Memorial Day parade, organized by American Legion Post No. 46, as they march past Chesamore Hall, is Warren Dodge. Others in the honor guard include Everett Dubray carrying the American flag and Everett Mudgett on the far right; others are unidentified. (Courtesy of Marie Boissoneault.)

A group of Boy Scouts and others observe the ceremony and listen to band music after the 1961 Memorial Day parade at the Whiting-Hill Cemetery. At this time, Hubert Beard was the Scoutmaster. In the background, across the river, Johnson Elementary School is proudly standing. (Courtesy of Linda Jones.)

Veterans of all national conflicts continue to be leaders of Johnson's annual Memorial Day parades and associated activities. Richard Parker, as commander, leads, from left to right, (first row) Wilmer Davis, John Thomas, Charles Patch, and Everett Dubray; (second row) Keith Bradley Jr. and three unidentified as they carry the colors through Lamoille View Cemetery. (Courtesy of the American Legion No. 46.)

Among the many contributions the American Legion Post No. 46 has made to the local area is its continued sponsorship of a state league baseball team. The post sponsored its first team in 1964 and continues this support today. Shown in the center of the first row is Legionnaire Farnum Emery with his assistants and members of the 1982 team. (Courtesy of the American Legion Post No. 46.)

The United Church float carried an organ and singers along the parade route during the bicentennial celebration. Included were Ida DeGoosh Barber, Marion Murray, Laura Green, Donna Boocks, Tammy Wells, Mary Bohn, Phyllis Jewett, Helaine Perkins, Nina Hooper, and Luther Hooper. At the organ are Clara Hopkins and Janet Bohn. (Courtesy of Helaine Perkins.)

Cub Scouts carry American flags as they march through Lamoille View Cemetery during an early 1980s Memorial Day parade. The Cub Scout troop was first organized in Johnson in the fall of 1955 and continues today. Pictured are, from left to right, (first row) Chad Blanchard and Timothy Percy; (second row) Christopher Jones and Timothy Sullivan. (Courtesy of Linda Jones.)

Girl Scouts were active in Johnson as early as 1948 with intermittent leadership over the years. By the 1970s, Brownies and Girl Scouts were again active with Susan Strong leading the Brownies and Judy Beard leading the Girl Scouts. At the 1976 Memorial Day Parade are, from left to right, Fawn Davis, Kimberly Beard, Gidget Dolan, Robin Strong, Martha Manning, Emily Locke, and Tina Strong. Leader Judy Beard stands behind her Scouts. Below, members of Troop 91, from left to right, Fawn Davis, Kimberly Beard, Susan Petrowski, and Robin Strong look out from a trail-side shelter during an eight-mile hike. Troop activities also included community service projects, mother-daughter banquets, summer day camp, and Girl Scout cookie sales. (Courtesy of Judy Beard.)

Boy Scout Troop 94 was organized in 1954 with 17 Scouts. A year later, the older Scouts formed an Air Explorer Troop and Cub Scouts were organized. Scouting has continued in town with many leaders and much community support. Boy Scouts enjoyed hiking and camping in addition to their badge work and community service projects. Pictured above at his 1984 Eagle Scout ceremony is Francis Sladyk (left) with Michael Jones. Below, other Scouts include, from left to right, Tony Lehouillier, Michael Beard, Scott Carbee, Brickett Bailey, and Ryan Bocock. These Boy Scouts remember overnight campouts every month of the year. (Courtesy of Judy Beard.)

Two

WORKING LANDSCAPES

Cloverleaf Farm, recognized as the first settled farm in Johnson, in 1784, is now owned by Alan Manchester. Despite the rocky, hilly landscape and Vermont's short growing seasons, this land continues to support agriculture today. Its location on the Hogback Road offers a spectacular view of Sterling Mountain as well as the meandering Lamoille River. (Courtesy of the Johnson Historical Society.)

No longer standing, this house was built by Benjamin Atwell in the 1830s. Located at 1000 Clay Hill, with agricultural land on both sides of the road, the farm was operated by Floyd and Evelyn Ellsworth for many years. The building was taken down in 2002. (Courtesy of Alan Beard.)

An early sugarhouse belonging to Floyd Ellsworth and located at approximately 1000 Clay Hill Road was destroyed in the hurricane of 1938. Steam can be seen escaping from the high cupola. On the left is a metal pipe that carried sap into the storage tank. From this setting one can see College Hill on the far left, known as the Despault Farm at that time. (Courtesy of Alan Beard.)

Long-time residents of Johnson, Floyd and Evelyn Ellsworth enjoyed dancing, perhaps at a kitchen tunk, after the farm chores were completed for the day. They were very active in community activities, including the Grange. Evelyn also participated in church activities and with Johnson's Home Demonstration Group. (Courtesy of the Mills Collection.)

The homestead of Frank and Annjanet "Nettie" Dodge, built on land at the northern end of Clay Hill in 1903, was known as the Mansion House. Like many Vermont dairy farmers, they also managed a significant sugar bush. The Mansion House offered a spectacular view of the Sterling Range including Mount Mansfield. (Courtesy of Alan Beard.)

Today Dodge's Mansion House Maple Syrup (above) at 3313 Clay Hill is a modern facility that produces organic maple syrup on the original Mansion House site. Maple sap is gathered from the trees using a plastic pipeline system known as tubing. Inside the sugarhouse (left), Frank Dodge checks his evaporator as the sap is being boiled. The Dodge family has a successful mail order business with products being shipped worldwide, including maple cream, maple sugar, coated nuts, ice cream topping, and several grades of maple syrup. Each spring, the family hosts an open house where visitors stop by to watch the process and to enjoy traditional sugar-on-snow and maple crème doughnuts. (Above, courtesy of Barbara Dodge; left, courtesy of Louise Cross.)

Built during the 1830s by John Burnham, the home remained in the family until 1903 when it was purchased by DeForest Collins. The farm was known as "the Willows" since there were two willow trees on the north side. A small pine tree, believed to have been growing from the time of construction, stood at the front of the house. The family farmed the land until 1947. (Courtesy of Jollie Parker.)

With horses hitched to the sleigh, Chellis Collins is probably ready to go down to the village. His home on Collins Hill was known as "the Willows." Even with this substantial pile of wood, Collins has told the story of how his family shared one downstairs bedroom during Vermont's long, cold winters. (Courtesy of Jollie Parker.)

Rev. A. Ritchie Low and his wife, Clara, bought the farm in 1947. Unfortunately, Reverend Low died in 1948. The home was vacant or seasonal until June 1963 when it was purchased by Everett and Jollie Parker and renamed "the Noble Pine." Many renovations were made. Through all the years, the pine tree grew to stand 120 feet tall until lightning struck it in 1971. (Courtesy of Jollie Parker.)

In September 1989, the home at 66 Parker Road became the "Homestead Bed and Breakfast," operated by Erwin and Ella May Speer. Over the years, many improvements were made. A small pine tree that grew where the noble pine had stood was dug up and given to the Parkers to plant at their new home. The business was a successful venture until 1998 when, due to health issues, the business closed. (Courtesy of Jollie Parker.)

Ken Hopkins and his father, Fred Hopkins, are standing in front of the family homestead at 833 Grow Road in the early 1900s. Known now as "the Windy Willows Farm," it continues as a sustainable agricultural enterprise. The homestead looks remarkably the same as it did in earlier years. (Courtesy of the Nichols Collection.)

On a summer morning, Jesse Hopkins, wife of Fred Hopkins, approaches the chicken coop to feed her flock of hens at Grow Road Farm. As was common at that time, she raised poultry to provide eggs and meat for her family's consumption. (Courtesy of the Nichols Collection.)

This sugarhouse on the L.R. Grow farm, near 833 Grow Road, is typical of early sugarhouses. The cupola on the top of the sugarhouse let the steam escape as the sap was boiled. The wooden trough system fed the sap into the sugarhouse. Wood was cut on the farm and used to maintain a fire hot enough to boil the sap. (Courtesy of the Nichols Collection.)

Sugaring is full steam ahead in early March. Buckets, first wooden, then metal, were hung under spouts which had been inserted into the trees for the sap to flow through. A wooden gathering tank on a sleigh was drawn by a team of horses. Ken and Clara Hopkins, in the 1930s, are ready to gather the sap. (Courtesy of the Nichols Collection.)

58

As years progressed, the wooden gathering tank was replaced by a modern metal one, however, horses continued to draw the sleigh. Note the pipe on the gathering tank, which could be lowered to let the sap flow into the storage tank at the sugarhouse. (Courtesy of the Nichols Collection.)

This picture of the Stiles Farm with several outbuildings and a view of its cropland, located at 275 Vermont Route 15 West, was taken in 1926. Later known as the Kenneth Hopkins Farm, the barns were replaced with one, large modern structure. It was always known to the family as the "old farm in Johnson." The property is now owned by the Laraway School. (Courtesy of the Nichols Collection.)

Haying was an important aspect of farming. Typical of the early 1930s, horses pulled the hayrack to the barn. The farmers used pitchforks to load the hay onto the hayracks. Important in the operation was the man on top, who placed the hay to balance the load and aid in the unloading process. (Courtesy of the Nichols Collection.)

"Up on the housetop to clean the smokestack. Yes sir, that's me." These are the words recorded by Kenneth Hopkins on the back of this picture in 1933. He is seen here cleaning one of his chimneys at the family homestead located at 275 Vermont Route 15 West. (Courtesy of the Nichols Collection.)

Pictured is an elm log, 44 inches on the end, which was cut on the land of Kenneth and Clara Hopkins. If it were two inches wider, it would be too big for the saw. Note the wheeled platform used to move the log through this 1930s era sawmill. (Courtesy of the Nichols Collection.)

In the 1930s, farmers made their own fence posts. Pictured here is Kenneth Hopkins with his father-in-law, Harry Stiles, sharpening fence posts with a circular saw at the family farm. Fence posts were a necessity in the pasturing of the cattle during the summer season. (Courtesy of the Nichols Collection.)

At 118 Lower Main Street West sits this large house with many sheds known as the Ned Holmes residence. He farmed the fertile land beside the Gihon River. Later, it was known as the Rhoda Sears house and presently is owned by William Jennison. It now houses several apartments. (Courtesy of Linda Jones.)

The Zachariah Whiting Farm, located at 1775 Clay Hill, was typical of most early farms with all the buildings connected. Several generations of Whitings lived and farmed here. The house and large barn still exist and are owned by Geraldine Whittemore, who operated a Morgan horse farm for many years. (Courtesy of Alice Whiting.)

This barn was located at 590 Rocky Road. The farm was purchased by William Sinclair in 1909–1910. In 1942, his son Lawrence took over. This 1960 picture shows the manure carrier, which brought the manure from the barn to the outside where it was dumped. The barn was taken down after the Sinclairs moved to the village in 1960. (Courtesy of Linda Jones.)

Standing in front of the milk house, farmer William Sinclair feeds his Jersey heifer a bucket of grain. Like many farmers, he raised Jerseys because of the rich fat content in their milk. On the upper right side of the picture is a track for the manure carrier, an innovation at that time. (Courtesy of Linda Jones.)

On the Sinclair Farm, a machine referred to as a "hay loader" picked up the hay and carried it to the top of the hayrack. Lawrence Sinclair is moving the hay from the loader to his father, William, who places it properly. Third-generation Marvin Sinclair, son of Lawrence, is holding the reins. Note the spoke wheels on the wagon. (Courtesy of Linda Jones.)

In the 1950s, some farmers used surplus Army vehicles instead of tractors. Another innovation was the hay baler, which made storage of hay in the barn more efficient. Riding on the hay load are Malcolm Mudgett holding his daughter Donna and Lawrence Sinclair. The house behind the load is the former Mudgett house, at 355 Rocky Road. (Courtesy of Linda Jones.)

64

A venture of Glenn Thompson's was raising strawberries, which he pedaled around the countryside in his 1930s truck. Local young people had the opportunity to pick fresh ripe strawberries for Thompson at 5¢ a quart. Local families enjoyed going to the berry patch to pick delicious fruit. (Courtesy of the Milo Collection.)

In addition to the strawberries, Glenn Thompson advertised and sold raspberry plants. Pictured here at his farm are several plants carefully packed, tagged, and ready for shipping. Most likely, he delivered them in his 1930s car to the train station in Johnson. (Courtesy of the Milo Collection.)

Local entrepreneur, Glenn Thompson inspects ears of corn, which became his popcorn (left). Grown on his farm at the head of the Hogback Road, it was sold locally as Bear Paw popcorn from the Depression era to 1968. After the corn was harvested, it was placed in the drying shed and later the dried corn was removed from the cob and packaged for sale. Many young people earned some pocket change by husking the ears of corn for 15¢ per bushel. Shown below, Thompson is explaining to his daughter Eleanor why it is called Bear Paw. (Courtesy of the Milo Collection.)

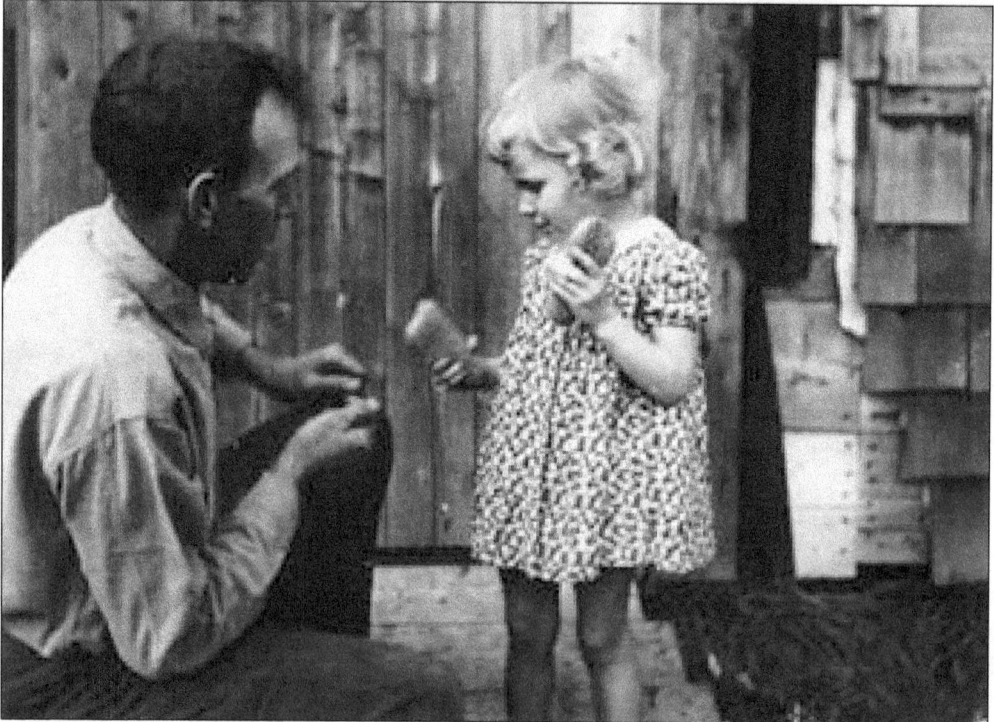

Harvesting ice was a winter chore for many farmers with ice considered the first crop of the year. Pictured are the various tools used in this manual operation. Note the tall stacks of block ice in the background. These would be transported for storage in an icehouse, then insulated with sawdust. (Courtesy of Linda Jones.)

In the early to mid-1950s, tractors replaced horses in many hayfields. Rita Audibert Lehouillier, as a teenager, is driving a Farmall tractor. Rita would have preferred to work out of town, however her father, Edgar Audibert, seen on top of the load of hay, needed her on the farm. (Courtesy of Rita Lehouillier.)

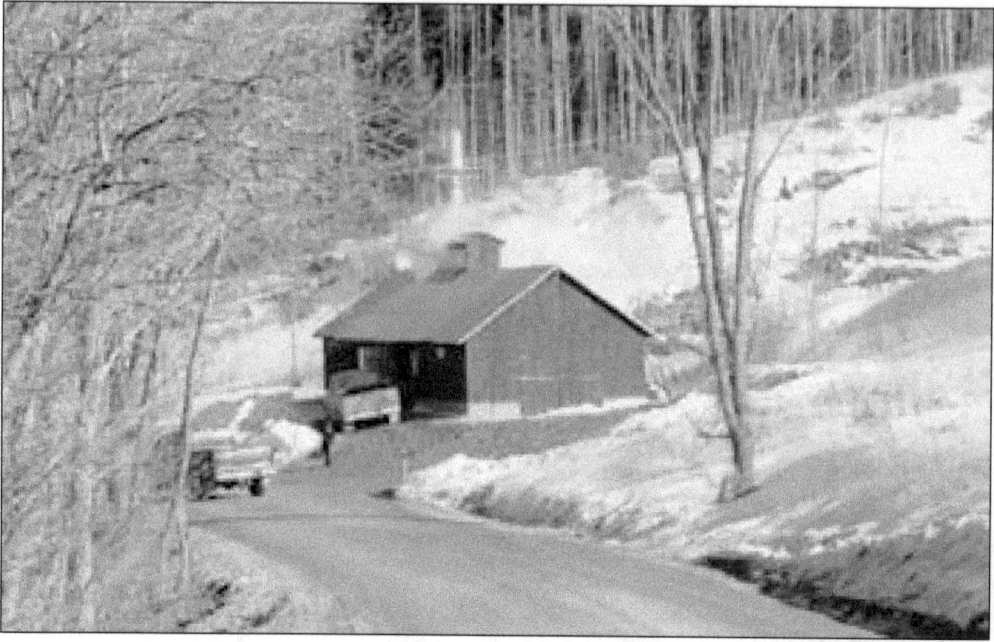

Springtime in Vermont could not come without being introduced by sugaring. This long-existing sugarhouse is located at 320 Sinclair Road and is operated by John Lehouillier with his son Rick (above). The sugarhouse and orchard was once a part of the farm of Joe Kittell and was, for many years, operated as a family enterprise. While introducing some modern technology to their operation, the Lehouillier family still prefers to use wood to fire their evaporator. Below, it appears Rick Lehouillier is about to add some wood to the fire as the steam rapidly rises to the exhaust cupola. (Courtesy of Louise Cross.)

This farm in East Johnson was home to the Roland Whiting family. Access is off Route 100C across a wooden bridge to 88 Gillen Road. The blower by the silo is ready for the corn silage harvest. This property is now owned by Johnson State College. (Courtesy of Robert Whiting.)

Steam rising from the sugarhouse on the Roland Whiting farm signifies that sap is being boiled down to make that delicious Vermont maple syrup. Imagine entering the sugarhouse feeling the moist air and smelling the aroma of the fresh syrup. (Courtesy of Robert Whiting.)

Using his bicycle to cross the pasture in 1952, Ernest Audibert, a sixth-grade student, checks the cows at his family's farm located in the vicinity of 1237 Vermont Route 15 W. The barn, like many in the area, was replaced following the 1927 flood. (Courtesy of Rita Lehouillier.)

Three

BUSINESSES AND INDUSTRIES

Assad Saleeby, shown here with his wife, Estelle, was born in Lebanon and came to America in 1892 at the age of 16. He started in business by traveling from house to house with a pack on his back selling his wares. Eventually, he opened a store in 1906 on Main Street where he sold high-quality clothing and foot ware. (Courtesy of United Church Collection.)

In 1912, Assad Saleeby moved the business to 50 Lower Main Street West and later purchased the building. Following the flood of 1927, the interior of the store was entirely rebuilt and new goods were purchased. The store had a broader selection including dry goods and ready-to-wear clothing. (Courtesy of the Mills Collection.)

The Nye Block, also known as "the Landmark," was built in 1869 by Leonard Knight. The three-story commercial building was more than 125 feet long on Railroad Street and 40 feet wide on Main Street. The imposing design caused many people to believe it was a hotel, not the mercantile establishment that met many of the needs for Johnson residents. (Courtesy of Linda Jones.)

This back view of the Nye Block shows its unique "flat iron" shape. The outbuildings were used to stable horses. The second and third floors served as a residence for the Nye family. Born in the building in 1904, daughter Mary lived there until the 1950s. The slate roof is credited with preventing the spread of the fire that destroyed the building in 1986. (Courtesy of Linda Jones.)

Standing beside the imposing Nye Block is the Johnson Lunch, which served lunch and dinner. It provided advertisement space for the Bijou and Tegu theaters in Morrisville. While the Coca-Cola sign is familiar, a classic Coca-Cola bottle is difficult to find today. This building formerly housed the Riddle Brothers, known for their sugaring utensils and tinware. (Courtesy of the Mills Collection.)

The Grand Union moved from the old post office building to the Nye Block. S&H Green Stamp signs are prominently displayed on this building. These green stamps were collected by many and were redeemed for household items. Houses beyond the Nye Block were demolished to make way for present-day buildings. The small structure near the street was Lower's bakery stand, famous for doughnuts and homemade bread. (Courtesy of Linda Jones.)

Looking down from Stearns Street and across the Gihon River toward School Street are the remains of the dam used by the Stearns Tub Shop to produce waterpower. The tub shop made butter and cheese tubs and was one of several active industries along this section of the river. (Courtesy of Marie Boissoneault.)

This 1945 photograph shows the dam and mill above the twin bridges in East Johnson, formerly called Perkinsville. In 1931, the mill had already been operated for more than 25 years by Charles Hayford to manufacture items such as wooden utensils and bowling pins. The dam was placed to supply waterpower to operate the mill. The building is currently used as a residence. (Courtesy of Linda Jones.)

C.H. Stearns Feed Mill, originally known as the Johnson Grist Mill, sits in the village on Pearl Street next to the Gihon River. As illustrated by this picture, a fire destroyed the building in the 1940s. The facility was rebuilt to satisfy the needs of local farmers. It is presently one of the historic buildings on the Vermont Studio Center campus. (Courtesy of the Mills Collection.)

A beautiful Jersey heifer at the age of 11 months and 25 days is displayed by D. Burleigh Smalley. The picture presumably was used to promote the value of feeding Whitmore Fitting Ratio, marketed by C.H. Stearns. He was the primary supplier of agricultural supplies to many local farms as well as coal for residential and commercial use. (Courtesy of Jon Gregg.)

Zillah Rexford operated the switchboard for the Bell Telephone Company from her home for many years. She had several coworkers as the switchboard was open 24 hours a day. The operators' voices were familiar to callers. When calls came in, the switchboard operator had to plug the cord into the appropriate slot. (Courtesy of the Mills Collection.)

Dr. Lyndhurst P. Holcomb was a member of the second class to complete a four-year course at the University of Vermont College of Medicine, graduating in 1906. Arriving in Johnson following graduation, he practiced medicine here for more than 55 years. In the rural tradition, Holcomb accepted maple syrup, potatoes, cordwood, and cuts of beef as payment. He is shown here with an early splint used to set a broken leg. His business card (below) calls attention to the fact that his practice included eye examinations. Note the limited hours, possibly because he was making house calls at other times. (Courtesy of the Johnson Historical Society.)

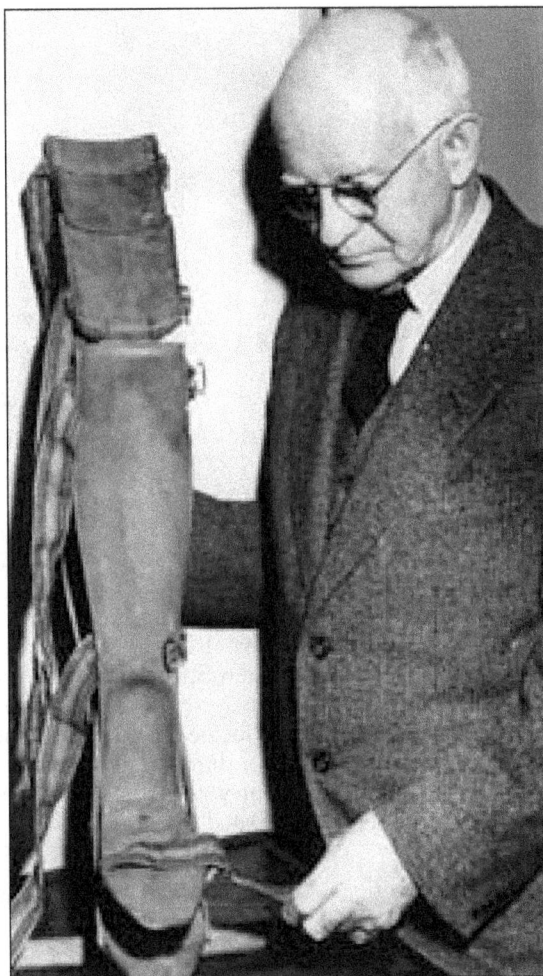

EYES EXAMINED
GLASSES FITTED

L. P. Holcomb, M. D.

JOHNSON, VERMONT

TELEPHONE
JOHNSON 26

OFFICE HOURS
1 TO 2 AND 7 TO 8 P.M.

Butternut Mountain Farms at 31 Lower Main Street East opened in 1986 and occupies two of the earliest structures on Main Street. The western-most portion of the building was the first house of Sterling Hose Company dating to 1895. Here is where Marvin's maple sugaring supplies and equipment salesroom is located. The eastern end was originally the yellow schoolhouse on Railroad Street and was later drawn to its current location to become Dan Scott's blacksmith shop. Today, it houses a country store that sells a variety of Vermont items, specializing in maple products. (Courtesy of the David Marvin family.)

The original Hotel Johnson structure was built by Capt. Thomas Waterman prior to 1812. The three-story structure closest to the street was added in 1887. It served as a social center in Johnson under various owners until 1936, when the town voted to go dry. The building was later purchased by Howard Hill, and it then housed retail establishments, rental rooms, and apartments. (Courtesy of Linda Jones.)

Several folks gather to view post-flood Main Street looking west. Cleanup has begun as one person is at work in front of the Hotel Everett. Also visible are the remains of a fuel tank that was floated to the surface by the floodwaters and deposited in the street. (Courtesy of the Milo Collection.)

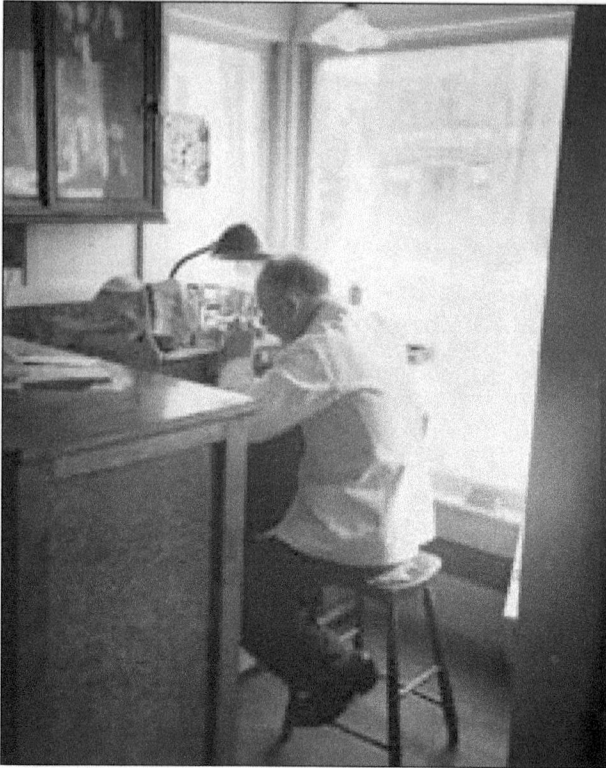

Dana Gilbert had a shop at 5 Lower Main Street West. Men could drop by for a haircut, shave, or beard trim. When not barbering he could be found sitting at his desk cleaning or repairing watches and clocks. At left, his work area is a case where he kept the repaired watches and clocks ready for their owners to pick them up. (Courtesy of the Mills Collection.)

Viewed from one of the hillsides behind Main Street, the building on the left is town hall. The small building beside town hall was at one time known as "the hearse house." Other buildings easily identified are United Church, Chesamore Hall, and the graded school. (Courtesy of the Mills Collection.)

This stately brick building at Two Lower Main Street West, believed to be built by one of the Watermans, became the home of Sterling Trust Company in January 1916. It housed commercial and professional office space. It was, for many years, the town clerk's office, home to S.R. Miller Insurance, and William Tracy, a lawyer. (Courtesy of the Mills Collection.)

Two prominent buildings have stood at 21 and 33 Lower Main Street West for many years. Shown here in 1925, one is occupied by Riddle Brothers and the other by C.P. Jones. Due to the similarities of the buildings' fronts, both are presumed to have been constructed by the same person. (Courtesy of Alan Beard.)

When Wayland Mills was a student in grammar school, a neighbor gave him a small camera as a birthday gift. This started him on a career of taking pictures of Vermont. As a young man working in the talc mine, he was injured and eventually lost his leg. When he opened his own photography service, he began getting films from nearby states and as far away as Florida. He provided complete photographic service including portraits. Many remember seeing him traveling around the community with two or more cameras and his cane. He recorded on film the day-to-day life and growth of Johnson. Many of the photographs in this book are part of his legacy, given to the Johnson Historical Society by his family. (Courtesy of the Mills Collection.)

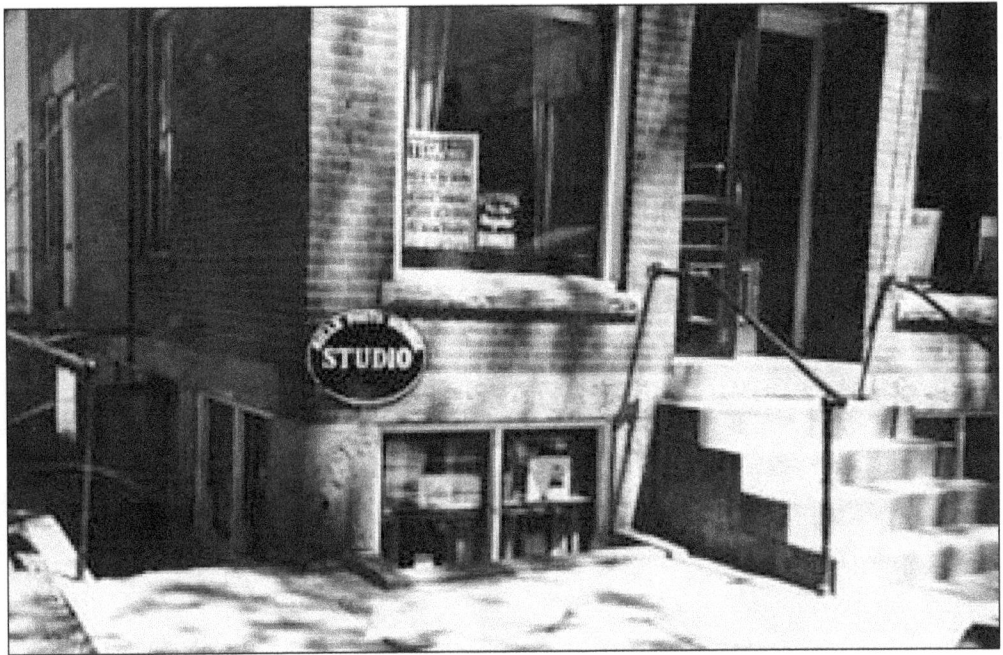

This brick building at 12 Lower Main Street West has served many purposes in the community. It housed the post office, the Grand Union, and various restaurants. Wayland Mills Photography Studio was on the lower level at the time of this picture. Later, a barbershop and then a beauty salon were in the same location. (Courtesy of the Mills Collection.)

In the 1940s, signs for the many Lower Main Street West businesses were prominent. These included Harold F. Beard Hardware, a dealer in Philco appliances, the Johnson Pharmacy–Rexall Drugs, the hotel building, and the partially hidden fruit store. Across the intersection is the famous Nye Block and Favreau's Café. (Courtesy of the Mills Collection.)

Hubert P. Beard's Hardware Store at 21 Lower Main Street West was the place to go for everyday and uncommon items. Hubert Beard took over running the store from his father in 1948. With his wife, Florence, and later his son Alan to help, Hubert operated the store until May 2007. (Courtesy of Alan Beard and Kindra Clineff, photographer.)

On the lower part of Main Street, sometime after the flood, a temporary bridge was constructed allowing traffic to resume delivery of goods and services via Vermont Route 15. The Muzzy building on the south side of the street had been moved enough to allow traffic flow. (Courtesy of Linda Jones.)

From Gould Hill looking over the Bishop henhouse and residence, several village buildings are visible. Moving up Main Street from west to east are three structures that no longer exist. The first building beyond the bridge is the Allen House, a stagecoach stop later known as "the west block." Beyond is a small garage and a building that housed stores and apartments. (Courtesy of the Mills Collection.)

As this c. 1920 car drives east on Main Street, it passes a stone watering tub and bandstand in front of the Masonic temple. Leaning against a tree by the bandstand is an advertisement for movies held locally. On the right of the street is the Raymond Green house with a widow's walk and the Orpha Whitney house. (Courtesy of the Johnson Historical Society.)

Richard Sinclair proudly stands in front of the new Grand Union. He started his Grand Union career at the former post office building at 12 Lower Main Street West. From there, the business moved to the Nye Block at the corner of Railroad and Main Streets before opening at this 115 Lower Main Street West site. (Courtesy of Linda Jones.)

The town fathers joined Richard Sinclair, store manager, for the ribbon-cutting and opening of the new modern Grand Union in the early 1960s. Pictured from left to right are (first row) unidentified, Richard Sinclair, and William Sinclair; (second row) Raymond Green, Roger Richards, and two unidentified. (Courtesy of Linda Jones.)

The Johnson Gulf Station at 221 Lower Main Street West was constructed on former pastureland in 1947–1948 by Sweet & Burt Company and was operated by Raymond Rexford for many years. Two subsequent proprietors were Charles Cole and Douglas Sargent. Shown in the upper photograph to the right is Douglas Sargent with David Frappier. Below, note the oil rack near the pump island, rarely seen today, as well as the windshield wash bucket. A close look in front of the gas pumps shows the bell-trigger hose line strung on the ground over the island to trigger the bell inside the station when a car drove up to the pumps. (Courtesy of Mildred Sargent.)

Looking across Pearl Street, this picture shows the Despault block (left, behind tree) that housed a store and apartments; the town garage (middle); and on the right is the Community League Gymnasium. Activities in the gymnasium included bowling, basketball, school dances, and physical exercise for all ages. (Courtesy of the Mills Collection.)

A typical scene on Stearns Street in the 1940s is the McLean family walking from school to their home in the apartment building that had been converted from the old tub shop at the top of the street. Shown is mother Melina with children Klan, Angus, "Chickie," Birdie, and Dale. (Courtesy of Marie Boissoneault.)

Albert S. Nadeau Aggregate Business was established in 1945 at 1908 Vermont Route 15 West. Due to shortages following the war, the super structure was built out of wood timbers. Seen in the photograph above, all the metal parts—such as crushers, screens, water pipes, and bucket elevators—were second-hand or from scrap yards. The Village Electric Department installed the electric wires and transformers. In 1958, a complete plant replacement was undertaken as shown in the 1959 picture below. The back of Albert Nadeau's house, which was built in 1948, can be seen behind the equipment. The plants continues to be family operated today as Nadeau Sand & Gravel. (Courtesy of the Nadeau Family.)

Aura Richards and sister Abby Dyke were proprietors of a general store located at 933 Route 100C in East Johnson. The first-floor store sold groceries to the surrounding neighborhood as well as gasoline for travelers along the highway. The sisters resided in an upstairs apartment. The 1946 photograph at left shows a large pile of wood for heating the store. Over the years, the building housed an antique shop, a rug store, and presently, it is the Winding Brook Bistro. The building on the left no longer exists. Below, Aura Richards is pictured with her birthday cake, sitting beside an old-fashioned radio that provided news and entertainment. (Courtesy of the Johnson Historical Society.)

The double bridge on Depot (Railroad) Street was carried away by the 1927 flood. Above, a couple with their horse and wagon return home from the village, perhaps after getting their weekly groceries. People on the south side of the river were unable to get to the village until this tram (below) was constructed. It involved a basket for carrying passengers and a hand-operated pulley system. The tram stayed in existence until the iron bridge was constructed. The houses seen are the Duba house on the left and the Choiunard house on the right, both of which are still standing. (Courtesy of Linda Jones.)

The temporary bridge across the Lamoille River, two miles west of the village on Route 15, was used to handle traffic after the 1927 flood. The newly formed ice above the bridge must have created another nervous situation for those responsible for maintaining the bridge. (Courtesy of the Milo Collection.)

The Rock of Ages cabins on the west edge of Johnson on Route 15 were actively operated for years by Martha Townley. The cabins were located on the north side of Route 15 at the base of the ledges coming down from Prospect Rock. Townley also operated a small store with gas pump across from the cabins. (Courtesy of the Mills Collection.)

The Oasis at 1442 Vermont Route 15 West was operated for many years as an inn for travelers passing through town as well as for vacations. The photograph postcard above was used to confirm the July 4, 1937, reservation for Mr. and Mrs. Dennison of Philadelphia, Pennsylvania, by proprietor M. Decill. Note a youngster playing in the yard and an adult sitting on the front porch. In earlier days, the Oasis property (below) was a working farm and continued that use while serving as an inn. The Ivan Stanton family, followed by the Claude Lehouillier family, farmed until the mid-1980s. Today, the Johnson Farm & Garden and Johnson Hardware and Rental businesses are operated there by Patricia Lehouillier and Alan and Lynn Lehouillier, respectively. (Courtesy of Linda Jones.)

Before modern snowplows were used to clear the roads, snow was packed down by snow rollers to make travel easier for horses and sleighs. These rollers were pulled by teams of horses. They were made from planks bolted to a drum-like frame. Rolled roads were wide enough to allow teams of horses to meet and pass without upsetting sleighs or sleds. The snow roller had the advantage of not leaving high snow banks. Above, Jessie Grow Hopkins and sister Emma Grow Reid are having fun on the snow roller at the Fred Hopkins Farm at 833 Grow Road, c. 1916. Note the seat for the driver when the snow roller was in use. Below, Roger Jones is on a different style snow roller. (Above, courtesy of the Nichols collection; below, courtesy of Linda Jones.)

The need for a connecting rail line between St. Johnsbury and St. Albans, Vermont, brought the good old days of railroading to Johnson. The town first voted to back the construction of the railroad by bonding at a town meeting in 1867. The first train ran through Johnson on December 15, 1876, and was operated as the St. Johnsbury and Lake Champlain Railroad. Steam engines (right) were the workhorses of the day with their string of freight cars approaching the station. At right, this photograph was taken as a train passes under full power through the rock cut east of the station near Dog's Head. Train service was vital to the growth of Johnson's industrial base. (Above, courtesy of the Johnson Historical Society; right, courtesy of Linda Jones.)

95

Throughout its history, the railroad was vitally important to the economy of Johnson. With several trains passing daily through town, mail and passenger service was offered. Also vital to the industrial economy was the freight service in support of the nearby lumber manufacturer and the shipping of finished talc products shown by cars on the siding at Vermont Mineral Company below. Dairy products, fertilizer, grain, and limestone were also carried by rail in support of Johnson's extensive agricultural community. Coal, used for heating by many homes, was supplied by rail service. Many locals remember taking the train to Morrisville and points beyond. (Above, courtesy of the Johnson Historical Society; below, courtesy of the Nichols Collection.)

Charles Bishop is shown hard at work as Johnson's stationmaster. In addition to monitoring trains, handling and organizing freight, and selling passenger tickets, the stationmaster was also the telegraph operator for Western Union telegraph service (right). People may remember riding in a railcar that was in part designed for passengers while the remaining section was occupied by mail service personnel busily sorting recently collected mail for efficient, rapid delivery. Passenger service ended in 1956. The St. Johnsbury and Lake Champlain Railroad was reorganized as the St. Johnsbury and Lamoille County Railroad in 1948; in 1978 it became the Lamoille Valley Railroad. In 2002, the tracks and ties were removed and the rail bed was designated for use as a four-season trail. (Courtesy of the Johnson Historical Society.)

Johnson's municipal hydroelectric power plant became operational in 1895 in the building located at the corner of School Street and Route 100C, seen here as it was originally built. The dam was designed to provide waterpower for the early turbine and may have been lost in the 1927 flood. (Courtesy of the Johnson Historical Society.)

The dam on the Gihon River provided power for both the woolen mill and C.H. Stearns. The 1816 deed provided water rights to both businesses. Waterpower from the river was used to wash the wool and power the milling machinery as well as grind the grain. (Courtesy of the Mills Collection.)

98

In the early days, Vermont was a sheep raising state. This is the original building that housed the woolen mill, established about 1836 by Andrew Dow. Local sheep farmers furnished the wool, which the mill processed into stout cloth. In 1872, this original building burned to the ground. (Courtesy of the Johnson Historical Society.)

One of the older buildings of Johnson Woolen Mill sits on the banks of the Gihon River. The water from the river was important for the cleansing of the wool. Some remember the changing colors of the river below the mill depending upon the dye being used each day. (Courtesy of Johnson Woolen Mill.)

The woolen mill was purchased in 1905 by Delmar A. Barrows, who added the present factory on Main Street and made changes in machinery and operation. The mill gained the reputation as "makers of the best wearing trousers in America." When Robert Barrows entered the firm in 1926, the product line was expanded to include clothing for all members of the family. (Courtesy of Linda Jones.)

Four generations of the Barrows family have been involved with the operation of Johnson Woolen Mill. D.A. Barrows, seated lower right, acquired the business from I.L. Pearl in 1905, taking in his son Robert, standing. In 1955, Robert's son Delmar Barrows, seated, became vice president and later retired full control to his daughter Stacy Barrows Manosh. (Courtesy of Johnson Woolen Mill.)

Harry C. Parker was born in Johnson. At the age of 24 he joined a partnership with Mr. Ober and Charles H. Stearns, which resulted in mills in East Johnson, North Hyde Park, Eden, and Hyde Park. The flooring and finishing mill at Johnson was built in 1909 and he purchased sole interest in 1917. Above, he is standing in front of Parker & Stearns dressing mill in 1920. Near the center of the picture below is a spark arrestor. This smoke stack is from the boiler where scrap wood, sawdust, and shavings were burned. A mesh cover at the top prevented sparks from spreading and causing fires. It appears that horses are being used to move the rail cars. (Above, courtesy of Jollie Parker; below, courtesy of Linda Jones.)

This picture is of an early Parker & Stearns mill in North Hyde Park. Workers are Edward Parker, Justus Foss, Arlo Wiltshire, Alden Hurlburt, Rossie Currier, Fred Heath, Frank Sears, Tommy Richen, Harry Page, Horace Farino, Clay Foss, Jack Amidon ,and the team of horses, Clyde and Dolly. (Courtesy of Linda Jones.)

In 1901, Harry C. Parker and Charles Stearns constructed a new mill in East Johnson. This mill manufactured lumber, bought logs, and dressed and sold softwood. In 1927, the mill was destroyed by the flood. This picture shows the destruction after the water receded. Subsequently, the machinery was salvaged and installed in the Johnson village mill. (Courtesy of Jollie Parker.)

Pictured is the complete complex of the Parker & Stearns finishing and flooring mill. Rough lumber from the sawmill was planed, kiln dried, and milled into flooring of hardwood species. It was graded and order-batched to be shipped primarily by rail. Today, the Manchester Lumber Mill operates on this site. (Courtesy of Jollie Parker.)

Parker & Stearns 1944

A major disaster in Johnson was the destruction of the flooring and dressing mill at Parker & Stearns in 1944. The Reo fire truck was located on the riverbank below the mill and pumped water continually to the other fire apparatus. Several fire departments aided the Johnson Fire Department for three days to contain this fire. (Courtesy of Jollie Parker.)

Johnson Fire Department was established in 1895 as the Sterling Hose Company as the sign indicates on the building at 33 Lower Main Street. Early volunteers of the hose company pose with their manpowered apparatus in front of the building that also served as a meeting room for several local organizations. (Courtesy of Mildred Sargent.)

Johnson's first fire truck, which was constructed as a pumper, was built on a Ford Model T truck chassis by "Rip" Reed of Morrisville in the early 1920s. It served the department until it was replaced in the mid-1930s by a new pumper built on a REO chassis. Notice the rear platform constructed to carry firefighters to fire scenes. (Courtesy of the Johnson Fire Department.)

There was a serious fire at Beards/Riddle Brothers Store at 21 Lower Main Street West in the late 1930s or early 1940s. The Johnson Fire Department used its REO pumper to fight the fire. The building was saved and served as Beard's Hardware Store until May 2007. (Courtesy of Bruce Beard.)

July 23, 1986, was a sad day in the history of Johnson. Main Street's Landmark Building, constructed in 1869, was destroyed by fire. The roaring blaze posed a very great danger to buildings close by, which were saved with assistance from several neighboring fire departments. (Courtesy of the Johnson Fire Department.)

The smoldering remains of the once majestic Nye Block/Landmark Building are viewed from the intersection of Main and Railroad Street. Clyde Stannard of Lamoille County Sheriff's Department manages traffic. The fire was ruled arson although a conviction was never secured. (Courtesy of the Johnson Fire Department.)

After more than 50 years of service, the 1935 REO was retired. This picture shows the restored REO on the day it returned to the fire station at 293 Lower Main Street West following eight months of restoration. The REO is used as the official parade and ceremonial unit by the Johnson Fire Department. (Courtesy of Johnson Fire Department.)

In 2004, the Johnson Fire Department lost its building and most of its equipment to a devastating fire. The REO was saved by cutting a hole in the rear of the building using a chainsaw, then pulling it out with a tow chain and bucket loader. Though badly damaged, the REO has been restored and continues to be the department's official parade unit. (Courtesy of Johnson Fire Department.)

The American Mineral Company founded the talc industry in Johnson in 1906. This photograph shows an addition that was made to the original mill after the mining operation was moved to a new site north of the village. Seen during the early 1930s, note the office and lab building, the railroad switch, and the background of the open hillside. (Courtesy of the Mines Collection.)

The head frame structure and hoist house at left were built about 1938. The low structure at right was built directly over the mine shaft opening. The structure, built at a 45-degree angle, contained the tracks for the skip as it exited the shaft. The skip unloaded at the top and the ore was separated into three sizes (coarseness). (Courtesy of the Bureau of Mines Collection.)

The hoist and electric-powered winch (drum) is used to raise the ore carrier (skip) from the mine shaft to the head frame. The hoist is located in a separate building from the head frame structure above the shaft opening. The marks on the horizontal board above the winch are used to indicate to the operator where to stop the carrier. (Courtesy of the Bureau of Mines Collection.)

Coarse ore is being loaded to one of the latest trucks used to haul ore from the mine to the mill. Note the two chutes to the left where the mid-sized ore was loaded. Hauling was still done by company-owned trucks until the mine was closed in 1983. (Courtesy of the Bureau of Mines Collection.)

The talc mill reached the peak of its production in the early 1960s. The mill and mine operations were employing 75 to 90 people. Note the original mine shaft in the left center of the photograph and the barn structures of the original farm once owned by Emile Fournier. The silo at the top right was a water reservoir for a sprinkler system. (Courtesy of the Johnson Historical Society.)

This 1947–1948 mine crew dressed for work includes, from left to right, (first row) Richard Collins, Wayne Bradley, Francis Byrne, Ralph Dubray, Jack Mitchell, Winston Dezaine, Luther Parkhurst, and Winfred (Buster) Dezaine; (second row) Victor Backels, Fred Dezaine, Cliff Allen, Robert Maxfield, Clair Nelson, and Roger Davis. Three of the miners are holding coils of dynamite fuse to ignite the day's charge. (Courtesy of the Mines Collection.)

This surface mine is as it appeared at the time of closing in 1963. Buildings were subsequently demolished and the remaining shaft opening was permanently sealed. Raw ore was then obtained at various out-of-town facilities until closing of the mill on December 16, 1993, thus ending a long chapter of Johnson's history. (Courtesy of the Johnson Historical Society.)3

This building, located on School Street, was constructed and occupied in 1950 by the Vermont Electric Cooperative on land purchased by the town in 1947 to induce the cooperative to establish its headquarters in Johnson. It previously had an office on Railroad Street. The original building (above) was built with brick. The west end section (below) was added to the building when the cooperative became a major dealer of Hotpoint home appliances in 1960. The appliance division sold its products to members with just two-percent interest and no money down with free installation. The appliance division was discontinued in 1976. The building remained as the administrative office until about 2006. (Above, courtesy of Alan Beard; below, courtesy of Vermont Electric Cooperative.)

From its first days in Johnson, the cooperative was managed by Walter Cook until about the 1980s. Shown from left to right are (first row) electric advisor Henry Parker Jr. and director Allan Wanzer; (second row) Jasper Sanville, Walter Cook, and Robert Leach. Cook was the creator of the cooperative's very successful appliance division. (Courtesy of Alan Beard.)

Four

EDUCATIONAL INSTITUTIONS

The Swamp School was located on what is now known as Swamp Road. It was one of the early one-room schools in town. Children of all ages in the neighborhood were educated here. In this 1886 picture, the lady in the striped dress is Alma Davis, the teacher. (Courtesy of Wilmer Davis.)

As one travels north on Foote Brook Road, Hillside School (left) is visible. Enrollment in this school varied with as many as 75 students in 1813. As the population fluctuated, the number of students increased or decreased resulting in the school's closure in 1943. Today, the building is a private residence. (Courtesy of the Mills Collection.)

Eleanor Thompson Milo and her cousin Janet are standing in the Thompson family's yard on a spring day in 1953. Behind them is the Riverside School located at the corner of Hogback Road and Prospect Hill Road. The school closed in January 1945, and the building is used today as a private residence. (Courtesy of the Milo Collection.)

Graded School, Johnson, Vt.

Voters in Johnson chose to consolidate village graded schools and high school in 1895. On the selected School Street site, construction of the first phase of the new school began. The Queen Anne styling is evident in the towers unusual ogee roof (above). The cost of the construction was $7,500. The first graduating class, consisting of three students, was in 1904. As more of the smaller one-room schools were closed, it became necessary to add an addition, which became the west wing. Pictured below is Johnson's graded school and high school as it appeared from 1911 through the late 1950s. (Courtesy of Linda Jones.)

High School, Johnson, Vt.

Dressed in formal attire with their high-collared dress shirts, the men of the class of 1918 pose for their picture outside Johnson High School (above). Pictured are, from left to right, Herschel Richards, Lloyd Fullington, Frank Sylvester, Howard Hill, Lewis Wood, Norman Scott, and Frank Sanborn. Years later, most likely celebrating one of their major reunions since graduating, they returned to the site. Below they hold the 1918 banner on the steps of their alma mater. Included in this picture are Howard and Ethel Hill, Norman Scott, and Floyd and Evelyn Ellsworth. (Above, courtesy of Linda Jones; below, courtesy of the Johnson Historical Society.)

Members of the Johnson High School Class of 1919 are, from left to right, (first row) Arthur Stiles, Harold Codding, and Paul Woodard; (second row) Mattie Fletcher, Evelyn Lambert, Amelia Chenette, Florence Brewster, Helen Waterman, Marion Barrows, Edna Gauthier, and Minnie Fletcher; (third row) Maella Bashaw, Madeline Fitzgerald, Amy Davis, Alice Davis, and Irene Westover; (fourth row) Ellis Parker, Ivan Leach, Leo Stearns, Frank Stiles, and Roy Cunningham. (Courtesy of the Nichols Collection.)

First- and second-graders posing on the front steps of the school around 1920 are, from left to right, (first row) unidentified, Robert Titus, Barbara Welch, Ruby Bennett, Stub Whiting, Max Archambault, Leah Coan, unidentified, Roth Poter, and Annie Archambault; (second row) Ila Jones, Isabelle Mills, Florence Perkins, Malcolm Newton, Wendall Hoisington, unidentified, Wilfred "Buster" Dezaine, and Benny Sewart; (third row) Parker McCuin and Raymond Whitney. (Courtesy of Isabelle Mills.)

The members of the class of 1930—including principal and teacher—are, from left to right, (first row); Geneva Bohannon, Ralph Bennett, Marion Hooper, Roger Jones, Ilda Jacobs and Beth Washer; (second row) Kenneth Allen, Principal, Claude Lambert, Lola McGinnis, Keith Stearns, Hazel Perkins, Kyle Jacobs, and Dante Amai, teacher. (Courtesy of Linda Jones.)

Students in the Johnson High School class of 1931 are, from left to right, (first row) Margaret Hines and Madge Hines; (second row) Ruby Davis, Edwin Whiting, Lorraine Munn, Erwin Davis, and Marion Collins; (third row) Isabelle Mills, Wilfred Dezaine, unidentified, Lloyd Lambert, and Frances Flanders. It is interesting to note all the white dresses and formal attire in this professional photograph. (Courtesy of Isabelle Mills.)

Standing beside the school is the 1940–1941 junior high class at Johnson Graded School, consisting of, from left to right, (first row) Paul Maynard, Wilmer Cook, Alvah Lowe, Betty Horner, Lorraine Coan, Nancy Rogers, Beatrice Bradley, and Flossie DeMerritt, teacher; (second row) Malcolm Franz, Richard Perkins, Geraldine Cameron, Nita Cunningham, Gene Sargent, and Wayne Brown; (third row) James Emerson, Roland Nadeau, Kenneth Horner, and Kenneth Adams. (Courtesy of the Johnson Historical Society.)

In 1942, a group of Johnson students conducted a scrap metal drive to aid in the war effort. On the Johnson school yard with Sterling Hall in the background are, from left to right, Charles Emerson, Junior Nadeau, Clyde Stannard, Curt Bradley, Junior Adams, Wilbur Ruggles, Lawrence "Pitt" Despault, and David Sargent. They stand surrounded by the metal they have collected. (Courtesy of the Nichols Collection.)

Basketball was a popular sport at Johnson High School. From left to right are (first row) Connie Perrault, Marylin Sears, Betty Davis (proudly holding the 1946 basketball), Marjorie Bradley, and Mary Kittell; (second row) coach Fossberry, Alberta Stannard, Beverly Rowe, Gloria Scribner, Dolly Messier, and Elizabeth "Babe" Kittell. (Courtesy of the Johnson Historical Society.)

In this late 1940s picture are, from left to right, (first row) Charles Frappier, Charles Hess, Paul Stannard, Dean Sinclair, Norman Currier, Boyd West, Charles Davis, and Austin Richards; (second row) Laura Lew Jones, Katherine Hooper, Dean West, Gus Wallace, Howard Russell, Marion Hopkins, Darlene Douglas, Faith Hoisington, Katherine Root, unidentified, and Ronald Russell. Note at least five of the boys are wearing Johnson Woolen Mill clothing. (Courtesy of Dean West.)

The 1953–1954 glee club members in the second-floor study hall at Johnson High School are, from left to right, (first row) Darlene Boyce, unidentified, Paula Sinclair, Laura Lew Jones, unidentified, Mabecca Horner, Kay Benway, Janet Dubray, Carol West, and Marlene Sweeney; (second row) Beverly Stackpole, Darlene Douglas, Eleanor Stewart, unidentified, Sandra McCuin, Janet Smalley, Eleanor Thompson, Marion Hopkins, Nancy Shattuck, and Doreen Stearns. (Courtesy of the Johnson Historical Society.)

Lillian Sargent, the teacher of this fifth-grade class, taught at Johnson for many years. The classroom with the big bay window was called "Miss Sargent's room." Included in the group are Janet Dubray, Carol West, Nancy Shattuck, Clarissa Hooper, Paula Sinclair, Sandra McCuin, Charles Kittell, Robert Mudgett, Dale Jennison, Mabecca Horner, and Gloria Gates. (Courtesy of the Johnson Historical Society.)

Toy Town Royalty was a money-raising event for the Johnson Parent-Teachers Association. The baby popularity contest royal results are, from left to right, (first row) duke David Perkins, duchess Monica Sargent, king William Perkins, queen Hope Miller, princess Eileen LeBlanc, and prince Paul Conger; (second row) Helaine Perkins, unidentified, Rachel Smith, and Arlene LeBlanc. (Courtesy of the Mills Collection.)

In the 1950s, some high school students produced minstrel shows. This one in 1953 starred dancers, from left to right, Carol West, Marlene Sweeney Sandra McCuin, Vicki Barrows, and Sylvia Sargent. The students in the back row are unidentified. These performances were held in the town hall to a full house of spectators. Some of the historic painted curtain is visible in the background. (Courtesy of the Mills Collection.)

"Good, better, best, never let it rest; 'til your good is better and your better is best." These words were often stated by Flossie DeMerritt. A graduate of Johnson Normal School in 1903, she taught in Johnson for 35 years. She was known for her discipline. She was active in her church and the Vermont Women Teachers Association, serving as president for two years. (Courtesy of the Johnson Historical Society.)

Three cheers for Johnson, no pom-poms, no skimpy costumes—but cheerleaders nevertheless, ready to cheer on the boys' basketball team in 1961. At the Johnson community gym they are, from left to right, (seated) Colleen McCuin Putvain and Linda Sinclair Jones; (standing) Sharon Byrne Grant, Bonnie Bradley Gray, and Annette Nadeau. (Courtesy of Linda Jones.)

The college traces its origins back to 1828. It was a normal school for teacher training in 1867 and become Johnson State College on July 1, 1962. Students attended classes in Chesamore Hall, pictured above. Later it served as the dining hall on the first floor with an auditorium in the upper level. Sterling Hall was built as a dormitory for the normal school in 1913, a three-story building to accommodate 24 girls. Later, in 1925, the first floor was renovated to provide a suite for a teacher plus a kitchen, dining room, and living room for the girls. Eventually, it provided an infirmary and housing for the school nurse. (Above, courtesy of the Mills Collection; below, courtesy of Linda Jones.)

Hill House was first leased and housed 19 girls in the early 1930s. The first floor had a suite of rooms for the housemother, a kitchen, dining room, and living room for the girls. Self-boarding students paid $1.50 a week for their rooms and a service charge of $10 per year to cover the cost of cooking fuels and use of equipment and rooms. (Courtesy of the Mills Collection.)

Known at one time as "Alumni House" on School Street and owned by the college, this building provided dormitory space for male students as well as housing for a faculty member and family. Now owned by Johnson Elementary School and known as "the Yellow House," it is used mainly for storage. (Courtesy of the Johnson Historical Society.)

McClelland Building was constructed and dedicated in 1941–1942. It was an administration building and it housed classrooms, a library, and a replication of a rural school with a stage and kitchenette. In addition, it included a bookstore, lecture room with projection screens, art studio, and large music room. Students attended classes in McClelland but returned to Chesamore for their meals. (Courtesy of the Mills Collection.)

On land that was formerly the Despault Farm, the first building erected on the upper campus was Martinetti Hall. Occupied in September 1959, it was built primarily as a women's dormitory on the upper levels with the main college dining hall and large auditorium room on the ground floor. This location was to become the main campus. (Courtesy of the Johnson State College Alumni Archives.)

This class is one of many Johnson kindergarten classes conducted by Johnson State College for one semester a year until the 1970s. Kindergarten was staffed and taught entirely by faculty and students of the college. Later, the program moved to Johnson Elementary School, with the teaching staff provided by the college. (Courtesy of the Johnson State College Alumni Archives.)

This Main Street building was erected in 1832 by the Congregational Society and was deeded to the town in 1854 as the town hall. In 1899, a stage was created and the building was host to high school as well as community functions, and it became known as "the Opera House." In the 1980s, the Vermont Studio Center purchased the building renaming it the Lowe Lecture Hall. (Courtesy of Vermont Studio Center.)

Visit us at
arcadiapublishing.com

www.ingramcontent.com/pod-product-compliance
Lightning Source LLC
Chambersburg PA
CBHW050641110426
42813CB00007B/1877